100 Teachings From Gita To Read And Reflect

Ananda

Dedicated to all those seeking growth and wisdom.

Contents

Ananda

Don't Skip

This book is designed to help you implement the wisdom of the *Bhagavad Gita* into your day-to-day life by reflecting on the teachings shared by Krishna. Now, I know what you might be thinking — "This asks really deep questions." But trust me, you already know most of these teachings. The challenge is not knowing — it's applying that knowledge in your everyday life.

This book is purely focused on taking what you already know and turning it into action. After all, knowledge is not power until it is used — so keep this in mind as you read.

I recommend reading one teaching at a time, ideally in one sitting. This allows you time to think, reflect, and connect the wisdom to your own experiences. There's a blank page after each teaching for you to write down your thoughts and reflections. I chose blank pages instead of ruled ones because many people prefer the flexibility. A blank page can be used for writing, sketching, or even pasting notes. For those who prefer ruled pages, I may consider releasing a ruled edition if there's enough interest.

In this book, Krishna's teachings cover all aspects of life. I wrote this because every morning, after waking up, I sit at my desk and read one shloka from thc Gita. I then reflect on it by linking it to my own life. Over time,

Ananda

I realized that many of us face the same challenge — we learn so much, yet struggle to apply those lessons in real life. That's what inspired me to create this book.

The format is simple and effective: each entry starts with a quote, followed by a short affirmation (which I suggest you read aloud), and ends with a reflection prompt to guide your thoughts.

I truly enjoyed writing this book, and I'm actively using it myself to reflect and improve. Why? Well, you'll understand once you finish reading — or when you reach the end of this book.

Enjoy your journey of reflection and growth!

Ananda

Emotional Well-Being

1.   **"For one who has conquered the mind, the mind is the best of friends; but for one who has failed to do so, the mind will remain the greatest enemy." – (Bhagavad Gita 6.6)**

Mastering my thoughts helps me stay calm and strong. If I lose control, my mind can become restless and harmful. Training my mind brings inner peace.

REFLECT: How can I train my mind to support me better?

2.   "He who is not affected by joy and sorrow, gain and loss, victory and defeat, is fit for liberation." – (Bhagavad Gita 2.38)

Remaining steady during both joy and sorrow helps me stay peaceful. Emotional balance frees me from unnecessary pain.

REFLECT: How can I develop calmness during emotional highs and lows?

3.   "A person who is not disturbed by the incessant flow of desires that enter like rivers into the ocean achieves peace." – (Bhagavad Gita 2.70)

Desires will always arise, but peace comes when I don't cling to them. Allowing them to pass like rivers calms my mind.

REFLECT: How can I practice letting go of desires without feeling empty?

4. "The wise man lets go of all results, whether good or bad, and is focused on the action alone." – (Bhagavad Gita 2.50)

When I focus on doing my best without worrying about results, I reduce stress. Letting go of outcomes keeps my mind clear.

REFLECT: Where in my life can I focus more on effort than results?

5.   "One who is equal in pleasure and pain, who remains steady and firm — such a person is fit for immortality." – (Bhagavad Gita 2.15)

Facing both pleasure and pain without attachment keeps me strong. Emotional steadiness makes life's challenges easier to handle.

REFLECT: How can I remain calm when faced with unexpected difficulties?

6.   "When meditation is mastered, the mind is unwavering like the flame of a lamp in a windless place." – (Bhagavad Gita 6.19)

A focused mind through meditation feels steady like a flame in still air. This calmness strengthens my ability to think clearly.

REFLECT: How can I build a consistent meditation practice?

7.   "He who is free from malice towards others, friendly and compassionate, free from possessiveness and ego, is dear to Me." – (Bhagavad Gita 12.13)

Kindness, forgiveness, and humility bring peace. Releasing negative emotions allows me to connect better with others.

REFLECT: What feelings of anger or pride can I release to feel lighter?

8.   "Perform your duty with a balanced mind, abandoning attachment to success or failure." – (Bhagavad Gita 2.48)

Performing my duties with focus rather than stress about success or failure keeps me calm. Effort matters more than outcome.

REFLECT: How can I stay committed to my goals without worrying about results?

9.   "Attachment leads to desire, and from desire arises anger. Anger leads to delusion, which results in loss of memory and wisdom." – (Bhagavad Gita 2.62-63)

Desire fuels anger, which clouds my judgment. Letting go of attachments keeps my mind clear and sharp.

REFLECT: What desires are causing frustration in my life?

10. "A person whose mind is unshaken by distress, who is free from longing, fear, and anger is called a sage of steady wisdom." – (Bhagavad Gita 2.56)

By detaching from fear, longing, and anger, I can maintain calmness. Emotional control allows me to act with clarity.

REFLECT: How can I practice patience when faced with stressful situations?

Ananda

Mindset & Positivity

1.   "Man is made by his belief. As he believes, so he is." – (Bhagavad Gita 17.3)

My thoughts and beliefs shape who I become. By nurturing positive beliefs, I can create a stronger, wiser version of myself.

REFLECT: What limiting beliefs can I replace with empowering thoughts?

2.   "You have the right to work, but never to the fruit of your work." – (Bhagavad Gita 2.47)

Focusing on my efforts rather than obsessing over results keeps me grounded. My mindset improves when I focus on what I can control.

REFLECT: How can I stay focused on my efforts without worrying about outcomes?

3.   **"The mind is restless, turbulent, strong, and obstinate; controlling it is as difficult as controlling the wind." – (Bhagavad Gita 6.34)**

The mind naturally wanders, but with patience and practice, I can guide it toward calmness and focus.

REFLECT: How can I improve my ability to calm my restless mind?

4. "No one who does good work will ever come to a bad end, either here or in the world to come." – (Bhagavad Gita 6.40)

Even if I can't see immediate results, my positive actions create lasting impact. Trusting this keeps me motivated.

REFLECT: How can I stay committed to doing good, even when results seem distant?

5.   "A person can rise through the efforts of his own mind; he can also be dragged down by his own mind." – (Bhagavad Gita 6.5)

My mind is my greatest tool — it can lift me to success or hold me back. Choosing positive thoughts empowers me.

REFLECT: How can I shift my mindset to become my strongest ally?

6. "Set thy heart upon thy work, but never on its reward." – (Bhagavad Gita 2.47)

When I focus fully on my work rather than rewards, I unlock creativity, purpose, and inner peace.

REFLECT: How can I shift my focus from results to the joy of the process?

7. "The wise see the same soul in a learned scholar, a cow, an elephant, a dog, and an outcast." – (Bhagavad Gita 5.18)

True positivity comes from seeing equality in all beings. Respecting others nurtures peace within me.

REFLECT: How can I practice seeing others with greater compassion and equality?

8.   **"Happiness that seems like poison in the beginning but is like nectar in the end is born of the purity of one's own mind." – (Bhagavad Gita 18.37)**

Difficult choices often lead to lasting joy. Short-term discomfort may be necessary for long-term fulfillment.

REFLECT: What difficult yet positive habit can I embrace to improve my life?

9.   "There is neither this world nor the world beyond nor happiness for the one who doubts." – (Bhagavad Gita 4.40)

Doubt limits my growth and blocks my path to success. Trusting myself and my journey opens the door to joy.

REFLECT: How can I replace my doubts with faith in my abilities?

10. "One who sees inaction in action and action in inaction is truly wise." – (Bhagavad Gita 4.18)

Wisdom lies in acting mindfully and knowing when to pause. True strength comes from thoughtful choices, not constant movement.

REFLECT: How can I create more moments of stillness in my busy life?

Ananda

Health & Wellness

1.   **"He who is temperate in his habits of eating, sleeping, working, and recreation can mitigate all sorrow by practicing the yoga of meditation." – (Bhagavad Gita 6.17)**

Balance in my daily habits brings physical and mental well-being. Moderation in food, rest, and activity keeps me energized and stable.

REFLECT: How can I improve balance in my eating, sleeping, or daily routine?

2.　　"The body is like a chariot, and the soul is its driver. The mind is the reins, and the senses are the horses." – (Bhagavad Gita 3.42)

Taking care of my body is essential for guiding my mind and soul. When my body is healthy, I can think and act more clearly.

REFLECT: What steps can I take today to strengthen my body as a vessel for my mind and spirit?

3. "Yoga is the journey of the self, through the self, to the self." – (Bhagavad Gita 6.20)

Practicing yoga aligns my body, mind, and soul. It brings inner calm and strengthens my physical well-being.

REFLECT: How can I include yoga or mindful movement in my daily life?

4. "One should lift oneself through one's own efforts and not degrade oneself. The mind is the friend of the conditioned soul, and his enemy as well." – (Bhagavad Gita 6.5)

Caring for my mental and physical well-being is my responsibility. By choosing healthy habits, I build strength and resilience.

REFLECT: What unhealthy habit can I replace with a better choice today?

5. "There is no possibility of one's becoming a yogi if one eats too much or eats too little, sleeps too much or does not sleep enough." – (Bhagavad Gita 6.16)

Wellness thrives on balance. Overindulgence or extreme restriction drains my energy and focus.

REFLECT: Where can I practice better balance in my lifestyle?

6.   "A controlled mind leads to a peaceful life, and peace brings health to the body." – (Bhagavad Gita 2.64)

When my mind is calm, my body feels lighter and healthier. Mental peace directly supports my physical well-being.

REFLECT: How can I calm my mind to improve my overall health?

7.   "By eating pure food, one's mind becomes pure; by a pure mind, one's intellect becomes steady." – (Bhagavad Gita 17.7)

Nutritious food nourishes not just my body but also my mind. A healthy diet supports clearer thinking and emotional stability.

REFLECT: How can I improve my diet to better nourish my mind and body?

8.   **"The senses are so strong that they can forcibly carry away the mind of a person striving for self-control." – (Bhagavad Gita 2.60)**

Uncontrolled cravings weaken both my mind and body. Developing discipline over my impulses strengthens my overall well-being.

REFLECT: How can I manage my cravings to create a healthier lifestyle?

9.   **"One who is free from attachment, who neither rejoices nor grieves on obtaining what is pleasant or unpleasant, is firmly fixed in perfect knowledge." – (Bhagavad Gita 2.57)**

Letting go of excessive attachment to comfort or pleasure brings mental peace, which directly impacts my health.

REFLECT: How can I practice detachment from unhealthy comforts that hinder my growth?

10. "The yogi, by meditating with a disciplined mind, becomes free from all impurities and enjoys the highest peace." – (Bhagavad Gita 6.27)

Through mindfulness and self-discipline, I cleanse my mind and strengthen my body. Peace comes from consistent practice.

REFLECT: How can I build greater self-discipline in caring for my mind and body?

Ananda

Time & Productivity

1. "Perform your prescribed duty, for action is better than inaction. Even the maintenance of your body cannot be accomplished without action." – (Bhagavad Gita 3.8)

Staying active and purposeful keeps me productive. Idleness leads to stagnation, while consistent effort drives progress.

REFLECT: How can I better manage my time to stay active and productive?

2. "The one who is unattached to the fruits of work and who works as obligated is the true renouncer and yogi." – (Bhagavad Gita 6.1)

When I focus on my efforts instead of outcomes, I avoid wasting time in anxiety. This mindset keeps me efficient and focused.

REFLECT: How can I focus more on my efforts rather than worrying about results?

3. "Even a small effort towards spiritual awareness will protect one from the greatest fear." – (Bhagavad Gita 2.40)

Taking small, consistent steps each day builds lasting results. Every action, no matter how small, matters in the long run.

REFLECT: What small step can I take today to improve my life?

4. **"Those who are deluded by the senses become attached to action and its outcomes, but the wise remain detached, performing their duties effectively." – (Bhagavad Gita 3.29)**

Emotional attachment to results wastes time and energy. When I focus purely on my task, I become more productive.

REFLECT: How can I create a routine that helps me stay focused on my work?

5. "The actions of a great man are followed by others. Whatever standards he sets, the world follows." – (Bhagavad Gita 3.21)

Leading by example encourages better discipline and focus in those around me. My time is best spent on actions that inspire others.

REFLECT: How can I become a better role model through my daily actions?

6.   **"A person who is disciplined in eating, sleeping, working, and recreation can mitigate all sorrow and stay productive." – (Bhagavad Gita 6.17)**

A well-structured routine fuels productivity. Maintaining balance prevents burnout and ensures consistent progress.

REFLECT: How can I improve my daily routine to enhance productivity?

7.   "The mind acts as both a friend and an enemy, depending on how it is trained." – (Bhagavad Gita 6.6)

Training my mind to focus on priorities helps me avoid distractions. A disciplined mind makes time management easier.

REFLECT: How can I train my mind to focus better on important tasks?

8.   "One who controls the mind and senses is free to focus on meaningful work without being disturbed by distractions." – (Bhagavad Gita 5.26)

By managing my distractions, I improve my ability to stay on track and complete tasks effectively.

REFLECT: What distractions can I reduce to improve my focus?

9.   "The mind, when controlled, leads to peace and stability; when uncontrolled, it leads to chaos and wasted time." – (Bhagavad Gita 6.26)

Time is wasted when my mind is restless. By staying calm and focused, I make better use of my energy.

REFLECT: How can I create moments of calmness to improve my productivity?

10. "One who sees inaction in action and action in inaction is truly wise." – (Bhagavad Gita 4.18)

Sometimes stillness and reflection are more productive than rushed efforts. Thoughtful pauses bring clarity to my decisions.

REFLECT: How can I improve my ability to pause and reflect before taking action?

Ananda

Purpose & Passion

1. "It is better to live your own destiny imperfectly than to live an imitation of somebody else's life with perfection." – (Bhagavad Gita 3.35)

Pursuing my own path, even with flaws, is more fulfilling than copying others. True purpose comes from embracing my unique journey.

REFLECT: How can I focus more on my own path rather than comparing myself to others?

2. "One who acts with devotion, free from attachment and ego, reaches the highest state of peace." – (Bhagavad Gita 5.12)

When I approach my goals with passion rather than pride, I find deeper satisfaction. Purpose thrives when my focus is pure.

REFLECT: How can I align my actions with a sense of devotion rather than ego?

3. "Better to strive in one's own dharma than to succeed in the dharma of another." – (Bhagavad Gita 18.47)

My true purpose is unique to me. Comparing my path to others only limits my potential.

REFLECT: How can I embrace my individual strengths and focus on my own purpose?

4.   "Perform your duty with focus and devotion, surrendering the results to the Divine." – (Bhagavad Gita 12.6-7)

True fulfillment comes from committing to my work without obsessing over results. Purpose grows when I stay dedicated without attachment.

REFLECT: How can I strengthen my focus on doing meaningful work instead of seeking instant results?

5. "Whatever action you take, do it as an offering with dedication and sincerity." – (Bhagavad Gita 9.27)

When I approach my work as a meaningful offering, it turns into something greater. Purpose blooms from dedication and sincerity.

REFLECT: How can I bring more sincerity and intention into my daily efforts?

6.   "That which is done without desire for reward, with a focused mind, is called true renunciation." – (Bhagavad Gita 18.11)

Letting go of the need for recognition allows me to focus purely on what I love. This mindset strengthens my purpose.

REFLECT: How can I let go of the need for praise and focus more on my passion?

7.   "By constantly remembering your purpose and dedicating yourself to it, success naturally follows." – (Bhagavad Gita 8.7)

When I keep my purpose in mind, my actions align with my values. Purpose thrives through mindful dedication.

REFLECT: How can I remind myself of my deeper purpose each day?

8.   "He who has no attachments, who engages in work for the welfare of others, attains supreme peace." – (Bhagavad Gita 5.3)

When I pursue my purpose with the intention of helping others, my passion becomes more fulfilling.

REFLECT: How can I connect my purpose to making a positive impact on others?

9.   "Your work is your worship — do it with dedication and love." – (Bhagavad Gita 18.46)

When I treat my work as a sacred offering, it becomes more meaningful. Devotion turns simple tasks into acts of purpose.

REFLECT: How can I develop a deeper sense of devotion in my work?

10. "The one who finds joy in inner reflection and self-discovery finds true fulfillment." – (Bhagavad Gita 5.24)

Discovering my inner self reveals my passions. Purpose grows when I reflect deeply and align with what truly inspires me.

REFLECT: How can I create more time for self-reflection to uncover my true purpose?

Ananda

Success & Achievement

1. "The one who is disciplined, who strives with determination and controls the mind, attains success." – (Bhagavad Gita 6.36)

Success thrives on discipline and mental control. Staying focused on my goals despite distractions leads to achievement.

REFLECT: How can I strengthen my self-discipline to achieve my goals?

2. "Abandon all attachment to the results of action, and attain supreme peace." – (Bhagavad Gita 12.12)

Focusing on my efforts instead of obsessing over outcomes helps me stay calm and productive. Success grows when I release anxiety about results.

REFLECT: How can I detach from the fear of failure and focus more on my actions?

3. "Success is achieved by those who are firm in purpose, patient in action, and unwavering in their efforts." – (Bhagavad Gita 2.14)

Perseverance fuels achievement. Staying patient and committed even through challenges ensures progress.

REFLECT: How can I build more patience when working toward my goals?

# 4.	"Even the most determined person's progress can be blocked by doubt. Overcome doubt with knowledge and confidence." – (Bhagavad Gita 4.40)

Doubt weakens my efforts. Gaining knowledge and trusting my abilities strengthens my path to success.

REFLECT: What doubts are holding me back, and how can I overcome them?

5.   "A person who does not let success inflate their ego or failure weaken their spirit is truly successful." – (Bhagavad Gita 2.57)

Staying humble in success and strong in failure keeps me grounded. This mindset ensures long-term growth.

REFLECT: How can I stay balanced regardless of success or failure?

6. **"Those who focus their mind fully on their goals, free from distractions, achieve greatness." – (Bhagavad Gita 8.14)**

Success requires undivided focus. Concentrating fully on my purpose amplifies my progress.

REFLECT: How can I create a distraction-free environment to improve my focus?

7.   "By dedication to one's work and devotion to one's purpose, success naturally follows." – (Bhagavad Gita 18.45)

When I put my heart into my work, success becomes a natural outcome. Passion combined with effort fuels achievement.

REFLECT: How can I develop deeper dedication in my current pursuits?

8.   "The wise do not get discouraged by obstacles; they adapt and continue their journey." – (Bhagavad Gita 2.14)

Success demands resilience. Obstacles become stepping stones when I embrace adaptability.

REFLECT: How can I turn my current challenges into opportunities for growth?

9.   "One who remains calm during both success and failure attains true wisdom and inner strength." – (Bhagavad Gita 2.15)

Emotional stability helps me make better decisions. Keeping calm under pressure strengthens my ability to achieve.

REFLECT: How can I practice staying calm when faced with uncertainty?

REFLECT: How can I practice staying calm when faced with uncertainty?

10. "Action is superior to inaction. Even the smallest effort leads to progress." – (Bhagavad Gita 3.8)

Taking action, no matter how small, keeps me moving forward. Consistent steps build lasting success.

REFLECT: What small step can I take today to move closer to my goal?

Ananda

Overcoming Failure

1.   "You have the right to perform your duty, but never to the results." – (Bhagavad Gita 2.47)

Failure often stems from attachment to outcomes. By focusing on my efforts, I can find peace even when results don't go as planned.

REFLECT: How can I focus more on my actions rather than fearing failure?

2.   "Do not be disturbed by failure; success often comes after persistent effort." – (Bhagavad Gita 18.78)

Every setback is a chance to grow stronger. Staying determined despite failure opens the path to future success.

REFLECT: How can I turn my recent failure into a learning experience?

3.   "A person who is steadfast in facing pain and pleasure alike is truly wise." – (Bhagavad Gita 2.15)

Failure loses its power when I learn to accept it calmly. Resilience helps me face life's ups and downs with strength.

REFLECT: How can I build greater emotional strength when facing setbacks?

4. "The wise do not grieve over what is lost; they focus on what can be gained." – (Bhagavad Gita 2.11)

Dwelling on failure drains my energy. Growth comes from shifting my focus toward future possibilities.

REFLECT: How can I focus on what's next rather than dwelling on past mistakes?

5. "Even the greatest of men fail, but they rise by learning from their mistakes." – (Bhagavad Gita 3.31)

Failure is not final. Learning from my mistakes equips me with the wisdom to improve.

REFLECT: What lesson can I take from my most recent setback?

6.   "Be fearless and pure; never waver in your determination." – (Bhagavad Gita 16.1)

Courage turns failure into growth. When I face setbacks with confidence, I strengthen my path forward.

REFLECT: How can I develop greater courage in challenging situations?

7. "The soul is neither born nor dies. It is eternal and unchanging." – (Bhagavad Gita 2.20)

My failures do not define me. My true self is far greater than any mistake I have made.

REFLECT: How can I remind myself that failure does not define my worth?

8. "Those who persevere in the face of obstacles will ultimately succeed." – (Bhagavad Gita 6.23)

Persistence turns failure into victory. Progress comes when I refuse to give up.

REFLECT: How can I stay committed to my goals despite recent challenges?

9.   "The mind that is controlled remains calm in both success and failure." – (Bhagavad Gita 2.48)

Emotional control prevents failure from overwhelming me. Staying calm helps me respond wisely to setbacks.

REFLECT: How can I practice staying calm when faced with failure?

10. "Defeat the doubts within your mind, and you will unlock your true strength." – (Bhagavad Gita 4.40)

Self-doubt magnifies failure. Confidence in my abilities allows me to recover faster and stronger.

REFLECT: How can I build greater self-belief to overcome my doubts?

Ananda

Relationships & Connection

1. **"He who is free from malice, friendly and compassionate, free from ego, is dear to Me." – (Bhagavad Gita 12.13)**

Kindness and compassion strengthen my relationships. Letting go of pride allows me to connect with others more deeply.

REFLECT: How can I become more compassionate in my interactions with others?

2.   **"The one who treats friends and enemies alike, who is calm in honor and dishonor, is truly wise." – (Bhagavad Gita 14.24-25)**

Balanced behavior, regardless of how I'm treated, helps me build stronger and more meaningful connections.

REFLECT: How can I practice greater calmness when facing conflict or criticism?

3. "He who sees all beings as equal in happiness and distress is truly devoted." – (Bhagavad Gita 6.32)

True connection comes when I treat everyone with empathy and fairness. Seeing others' struggles helps me build deeper bonds.

REFLECT: How can I be more understanding of others' feelings and experiences?

4.   "A person who neither praises nor criticizes others remains peaceful and content." – (Bhagavad Gita 12.19)

Avoiding gossip and judgment nurtures harmony. Choosing kindness over criticism strengthens my relationships.

REFLECT: How can I speak more positively about others?

5.   "Those who conquer anger and hatred remain steady in their relationships." – (Bhagavad Gita 5.26)

Controlling my emotions helps me maintain calm and resolve conflicts peacefully.

REFLECT: How can I respond with calmness when I feel hurt or frustrated?

6.   "He who is patient, forgiving, and self-controlled is truly strong." – (Bhagavad Gita 16.1-2)

Patience and forgiveness are essential for lasting relationships. Letting go of grudges brings peace.

REFLECT: How can I practice forgiveness to improve my relationships?

7. "By renouncing pride and selfishness, one earns the love and trust of others." – (Bhagavad Gita 3.30)

Humility and selflessness strengthen my bonds with people. Letting go of ego creates space for genuine connection.

REFLECT: How can I let go of my ego to build stronger relationships?

8. "Those who find joy in serving others live a life of true fulfillment." – (Bhagavad Gita 3.25)

Relationships thrive when I give without expecting anything in return. Service creates lasting connections.

REFLECT: How can I be more giving and selfless in my relationships?

9. "The one who sees the Divine in every being treats all with love and respect." – (Bhagavad Gita 5.18)

Recognizing the value of every individual brings harmony to my connections. Respect deepens my bonds.

REFLECT: How can I show greater respect and kindness to the people around me?

10. "Those who avoid envy and celebrate the success of others live with greater joy." – (Bhagavad Gita 12.15)

Celebrating others' achievements brings positivity to my relationships. Gratitude and encouragement foster stronger connections.

REFLECT: How can I be more joyful about others' success without comparison?

Ananda

Leadership & Influence

1.   "Whatever a great person does, others follow. Whatever standards they set, others adopt." – (Bhagavad Gita 3.21)

Leading by example shapes those around me. My actions influence more than my words.

REFLECT: How can I become a better role model through my actions?

2.   **"The wise guide others without pride or attachment, inspiring by example." – (Bhagavad Gita 3.25)**

True leaders uplift others with humility. Inspiring by action builds lasting influence.

REFLECT: How can I lead with humility and inspire others naturally?

3. "One who performs their duty without selfish motives earns the trust and respect of others." – (Bhagavad Gita 3.19)

Genuine leadership comes from working selflessly, placing purpose before personal gain.

REFLECT: How can I focus more on serving others while leading?

4. "A leader should not unsettle the minds of those who are attached to action but guide them wisely." – (Bhagavad Gita 3.26)

Effective leaders understand people's limitations and guide them patiently. Forcing change creates resistance.

REFLECT: How can I guide others with patience rather than pressure?

5.   "One who is tolerant, forgiving, and calm becomes a natural leader." – (Bhagavad Gita 12.15)

Patience and forgiveness create trust. Calmness helps me inspire confidence in others.

REFLECT: How can I remain calm and patient when leading others?

6.   "The one who controls their senses and mind is a true leader." – (Bhagavad Gita 5.7)

Leadership starts with self-control. Managing my thoughts and emotions allows me to influence others positively.

REFLECT: How can I develop better control over my emotions to lead more effectively?

7. "One who is firm in truth, committed to justice, and free from deceit is a true leader." – (Bhagavad Gita 16.2)

Integrity earns respect. Being honest and fair strengthens my influence.

REFLECT: How can I uphold truth and fairness in my leadership style?

8.   "By serving others without pride, one becomes truly powerful." – (Bhagavad Gita 13.8)

Serving without arrogance creates deeper influence. People trust those who act with sincerity.

REFLECT: How can I lead with more humility and service?

9.   "The one who sees no difference between themselves and others acts with compassion and leads with wisdom." – (Bhagavad Gita 6.32)

Empathy allows me to connect with those I lead. Understanding others' struggles builds trust.

REFLECT: How can I develop greater empathy to guide others better?

10. "One who remains unshaken in success and failure inspires others with their stability." – (Bhagavad Gita 2.15)

Consistency in difficult times shows true leadership. Calmness during adversity encourages others to stay strong.

REFLECT: How can I stay grounded when facing challenges as a leader?

Ananda

Spiritual Growth & Gratitude

1. **"He who is content with what comes by chance, who is free from envy, and steady in both success and failure, is truly peaceful." – (Bhagavad Gita 4.22)**

Gratitude grows when I accept life's outcomes without comparison or resentment. Inner peace comes from embracing what I have.

REFLECT: How can I develop deeper contentment with what I already have?

2.   "The mind that is calm, focused, and free from desires finds true joy within itself." – (Bhagavad Gita 6.20)

Lasting happiness comes from inner peace, not external achievements. Spiritual growth begins by seeking stillness within.

REFLECT: How can I create more moments of inner calm in my life?

3.   "That person is truly wise who sees the same Divine presence in all beings — be they kind, cruel, rich, or poor." – (Bhagavad Gita 5.18)

Gratitude flourishes when I recognize the value in everyone. Seeing unity in all beings nurtures compassion.

REFLECT: How can I practice seeing the Divine in everyone I meet?

4.   "By offering all actions to the Divine, one finds true freedom from worry and regret." – (Bhagavad Gita 5.10)

Surrendering my actions to a higher purpose relieves me from stress. Gratitude deepens when I let go of control.

REFLECT: How can I focus more on giving my best without attachment to results?

5.   "The truly wise seek the eternal, not the temporary, and are content in their inner self." – (Bhagavad Gita 2.69)

Chasing fleeting desires brings unrest. Spiritual growth thrives when I prioritize inner peace over material gain.

REFLECT: How can I focus more on lasting fulfillment rather than short-term pleasures?

6.   "He who accepts both praise and blame with equal calmness is truly mature." – (Bhagavad Gita 12.19)

Embracing both appreciation and criticism with balance helps me grow stronger. Gratitude builds when I accept life's feedback peacefully.

REFLECT: How can I become more accepting of both praise and criticism?

7. "The soul is eternal, unaffected by birth or death, untouched by pain or pleasure." – (Bhagavad Gita 2.20)

Spiritual strength grows when I recognize that my inner self is unshaken by life's ups and downs.

REFLECT: How can I remind myself that my true self is beyond temporary struggles?

8.   "Renounce pride and embrace humility; this leads to inner peace and spiritual growth." – (Bhagavad Gita 13.8)

Letting go of pride creates space for gratitude. Humility strengthens my connection with the world.

REFLECT: How can I practice greater humility in my daily life?

9. "Even a little spiritual practice protects one from great danger and brings peace." – (Bhagavad Gita 2.40)

Small steps toward mindfulness or prayer can create lasting calmness and strength.

REFLECT: What small spiritual practice can I include in my routine to feel more grounded?

10. "The one who is grateful for everything, whether big or small, lives with true abundance." – (Bhagavad Gita 17.16)

Gratitude isn't just about grand moments; it's about finding joy in life's simplest blessings.

REFLECT: How can I better appreciate the small joys in my daily life?

Ananda

Conclusion

I just want to say — if you're reading this, there's a high probability that you enjoyed this book and now wonder, "What's next?" The simple answer is — this book again.

As the saying goes, "A man never steps into the same river twice; both the man and the river have changed." The next time you revisit this book — whether right after now or sometime later in life — you won't be the same person you were when you started this journey. Each time you read it, new insights may surface, and you'll reflect from a different perspective.

So, whenever you're ready — dive back in, and embrace the wisdom anew

Ananda

Acknowledgement

I would like to express my deepest gratitude to **A.C. Bhaktivedanta Swami Prabhupada** for translating and writing the *Bhagavad Gita As It Is*. His work has been an invaluable guide in helping me understand Krishna's teachings and apply them in my life. The wisdom he shared has transformed my perspective in every dimension — spiritually, mentally, and emotionally. Without his dedicated efforts to bring Krishna's words to the world, this book would not have been possible.

Thank you for illuminating the path of self-realization and inspiring countless seekers like me to walk it with faith and understanding.

Ananda – The Ultimate Happiness

Ananda